Living Lenormand

Copyright © 2025 by Night Willow Oracle

All rights reserved. No part of this book may be reproduced in any form without permission from the publisher.

Published by Night Willow Oracle
etsy.com/shop/NightWillowOracle
NightWillowOracle.com

Welcome to the world of Lenormand cards, a 36-card divination system that uses simple, direct symbols to create clear and practical readings.

This book is a companion to the *Learning Lenormand* deck, offering a deeper exploration of the 36 Lenormand cards and their meanings. Here you'll find expanded meanings for each card, helping you refine your readings with clarity and confidence.

A dedicated section of this book covers the basics of reading Lenormand, making it easy for beginners to get started, while another section explores cards with similar meanings and how to distinguish their nuances in a spread.

To further enhance your skills, eight sample readings demonstrate how to weave the cards together for insightful and accurate interpretations.

Whether you're new to Lenormand or looking to sharpen your abilities, Learning Lenormand provides the tools you need to master this dynamic divination system.

TABLE OF CONTENTS

1 - Rider 6

2 - Clover 8

3 - Ship 10

4 - House 12

5 - Tree 14

6 - Clouds 16

7 - Snake 18

8 - Coffin 20

9 - Bouquet 22

10 - Scythe 24

11 - Whip 26

12 - Birds 28

13 - Child 30

14 - Fox 32

15 - Bear 34

16 - Stars 36

17 - Stork 38

18 - Dog 40

19 - Tower 42

20 - Garden 44

TABLE OF CONTENTS

21 - Mountain 46

22 - Path..48

23 - Mice 50

24 - Heart 52

25 - Ring 54

26 - Book 56

27 - Letter 58

28 - Man... 60

29 - Woman 62

30 - Lily 64

31 - Sun 66

32 - Moon 68

33 - Key 70

34 - Fish... 72

35 - Anchor 74

36 - Cross 76

Basics of Lenormand Reading 79

Reading Card Pairs 83

Cards With Similarities 85

Sample Two-Card Readings 95

1 Rider

Fast Progress | Visitor | Arrival
Delivery | Message | Speed | News
New Direction | Action | Energy

1 Rider

> Fast Progress | Visitor | Arrival
> Delivery | Message | Speed | News
> New Direction | Action | Energy

The Rider card is all about movement, news, and things happening quickly. When this card shows up, it's like a messenger arriving with important updates or fresh energy. You might be stepping into a period where things start to move quickly, whether it's a new project, an unexpected event, or a chance to pursue something exciting. Pay attention to what's coming your way—it's likely something that can spark change or set things in motion.

You'll want to stay open and alert because the Rider can represent fast-paced developments. Whether it's a person bringing you information or a situation gaining momentum, this card often signals the need to act or respond promptly. Think of it as a wake-up call to engage with what's ahead rather than standing still.

At its core, the Rider encourages you to embrace progress and movement. It's a reminder to seize opportunities and stay adaptable as things unfold. If you've been waiting for a green light, this card might just be it, so get ready to move forward with confidence and curiosity.

2 Clover

Luck | Opportunity | Serendipity
Good Fortune | Chance | Playfulness
Lightheartedness | Optimism

2 Clover

> Luck | Opportunity | Serendipity
> Good Fortune | Chance | Playfulness
> Lightheartedness | Optimism

The Clover card is all about luck, opportunities, and those moments of good fortune that seem to pop up out of nowhere. When this card shows up, it signals that something positive may be just around the corner, but it's often fleeting, so you'll need to be ready to seize the moment. Stay open and receptive, because sometimes life brings you a lucky break when you least expect it.

The Clover also represents a carefree and playful energy. It suggests that you don't need to take things too seriously right now. Instead, enjoy the small wins and the happy coincidences that come your way. Approach situations with optimism and a sense of fun, which can help you notice opportunities you might otherwise miss.

However, the Clover's luck tends to be short-lived, so while it brings good things, it also reminds you not to rely on chance alone. Take advantage of the luck while it's there, but don't count on it sticking around forever. Stay proactive, catch the moment, and enjoy the burst of fortune that comes your way.

3 Ship

Adventure | Expansion | Departure
Journey | Exploration | New Horizons
Distance | Progress | Travel

3 Ship

> Adventure | Expansion | Departure
> Journey | Exploration | New Horizons
> Distance | Progress | Travel

The Ship card is all about journeys, both literal and metaphorical. When this card appears, it signals movement, change, or travel—whether you're physically planning a trip or navigating a transition in your life. It can encourage you to explore new horizons, take a risk, or set your sights on a new goal. If you've been feeling stuck, the Ship invites you to look beyond your current situation and consider what opportunities are waiting for you just over the horizon.

On a deeper level, the Ship also symbolizes the flow of energy and emotions. Just as a ship travels with the current of the sea, you're being encouraged to go with the flow in your life. This card suggests that now is a good time to follow your instincts and let things unfold naturally, rather than trying to control every outcome.

In practical terms, the Ship card can represent a need for expansion, whether that's in your career, relationships, or personal growth. It urges you to leave your comfort zone and see what the world has to offer, suggesting that the best is yet to come as long as you're open to change and new experiences.

4 House

Home | Family | Security
Foundation | Tradition | Shelter
Safety | Personal Boundaries

4 House

> Home | Family | Security
> Foundation | Tradition | Shelter
> Safety | Personal Boundaries

The House card represents home, family, and a sense of comfort. It's all about stability and the familiar—the place or people that make you feel safe and grounded. When this card appears, it often points to issues related to your personal life, living situation, or those close to you. It highlights the importance of your home base, whether that's your physical space or emotional support network.

Beyond just your physical house, this card symbolizes security and foundations. It's about creating a solid structure in your life, where you can retreat and recharge. The House also suggests traditions and routines, reminding you that some aspects of life benefit from predictability and consistency. It's a card of roots, indicating that your foundation is strong and reliable.

The House can also reflect matters of privacy or personal boundaries. It's a reminder to protect your space, both physically and emotionally. Whether you're focusing on relationships, career, or personal well-being, focus on maintaining a secure and stable environment where you feel supported and grounded.

5 Tree

Development | Nature | Ancestry
Well-Being | Longevity | Endurance
Growth | Health | Stability | Roots

5 Tree

Development | Nature | Ancestry
Well-Being | Longevity | Endurance
Growth | Health | Stability | Roots

The Tree card reflects the foundation of health—both physical and emotional—as well as long-term development. When the Tree appears, it often points to something that has deep roots, whether that's your health, family, or a developing situation. It's about slow and steady growth, indicating that patience and nurturing are key elements.

In a broader sense, the Tree can symbolize connections and the way your life branches out into different areas, such as your relationships, career, or personal growth. Just like a tree, your life has various aspects that require balance and attention to thrive. This card suggests that everything is interconnected, and the strength of your "roots" will determine how well you can withstand challenges.

The Tree also carries connotations of longevity and endurance. It's a reminder that some things take time to grow and develop, but with the right care, they'll flourish. Whether it's focusing on your health, your spiritual path, or long-term goals, the Tree encourages you to stay committed and trust the process of natural growth.

6 Clouds

Confusion | Uncertainty | Hesitation
Doubt | Ambiguity | Misunderstanding
Complication | Mental Fog

6 Clouds

Confusion | Uncertainty | Hesitation
Doubt | Ambiguity | Misunderstanding
Complication | Mental Fog

When you see the Clouds card, it signals that things may feel a bit murky right now. You're not seeing the full picture, and decision-making might be difficult because of it. Just like a cloudy sky blocks the sun, the Clouds card suggests that you may be struggling with doubts, indecision, or misunderstandings. It's a time when things feel unclear, and you might be left wondering which direction to take.

This card often points to temporary problems or complications that obscure the truth. It reflects turbulent situations where the answers you're seeking are just out of reach. Confusion or instability is impacting your thinking, making it harder to find a solution or see things clearly. Have patience. Wait for the clouds to pass so clarity can return.

However, the Clouds card also serves as a reminder that, like real clouds, this confusion will eventually clear. While you might feel lost or uncertain now, the fog will lift, and with time, you'll gain a better understanding of your situation. Until then, it's important to avoid acting impulsively or making hasty decisions.

7 Snake

Deception | Betrayal | Temptation
Hidden Agenda | Deceit | Seduction
Being Blindsided | Manipulation

7 Snake

> Deception | Betrayal | Temptation
> Hidden Agenda | Deceit | Seduction
> Being Blindsided | Manipulation

When you encounter the Snake, it's a reminder to pay attention to the motives of those around you. Everything may not be as it appears; hidden agendas or complicated emotions may be at play. Whether it's in relationships, work situations, or personal interactions, look beneath the surface and be wary of any tempting offers that may lead you astray.

In relationships, the Snake can warn of potential betrayal or manipulation. If you're sensing that someone isn't being entirely honest, the Snake encourages you to trust your instincts and dig a little deeper. Someone may be trying to lure you into a situation that feels enticing but could ultimately lead to complications.

When it comes to decision-making, consider the complexities of your choices and to be aware of any risks. By being vigilant and discerning, you can navigate tricky situations more effectively. Ultimately, the Snake card emphasizes the importance of clarity and transparency in all areas of life.

8 Coffin

Endings | Loss | Grief
Transition | Release of the Past
Letting Go | Transformation

8 Coffin

> Endings | Loss | Grief
> Transition | Release of the Past
> Letting Go | Transformation

While it can initially evoke feelings of loss or grief, the deeper message of the Coffin is about the necessary process of letting go to make way for new beginnings. When this card appears in a reading, it often indicates that something in your life is coming to an end—this could be a relationship, a job, or even a way of thinking that no longer serves you.

In a personal context, reflect on what you might need to release. Holding onto the past can prevent you from moving forward. Embracing the idea of closure allows you to heal and create space for new opportunities. This card encourages you to acknowledge your feelings about the ending but also to recognize the potential for transformation that lies ahead.

Additionally, the Coffin can represent a period of introspection and self-discovery. It prompts you to dive deep into your inner world, confront any lingering issues, and allow yourself to process emotions. Ultimately, the Coffin signifies that while endings can be challenging, they are often the catalysts for fresh starts and new chapters in life.

9 Bouquet

Joy | Gratitude | Beauty
Pleasant Surprises | Gifts | Kindness
Positive Emotions | Appreciation

9 Bouquet

> Joy | Gratitude | Beauty
> Pleasant Surprises | Gifts | Kindness
> Positive Emotions | Appreciation

The Bouquet card is all about positivity, beauty, and appreciation. When this card shows up, it's a signal to embrace the good things in life and acknowledge the blessings around you. It often represents pleasant surprises, gifts, or moments of recognition that bring happiness. You might find yourself at the center of attention or receiving an unexpected compliment or opportunity.

This card is a reminder to appreciate not only what you receive but also what you can offer to others. Think of it as an invitation to share kindness, whether through a thoughtful gesture, a kind word, or simply showing gratitude. It's about creating an atmosphere of positivity and warmth that uplifts everyone involved.

On a deeper level, the Bouquet encourages you to celebrate the beauty in the present moment. Whether it's finding joy in small pleasures or acknowledging the people who brighten your life, this card invites you to cultivate a sense of appreciation and harmony. Life blooms when you focus on what's lovely and worthwhile.

10 Scythe

Sudden Change | Immediate Action
Accident | Quick Decision | Severance
Swift Resolution | Breaking Free

10 Scythe

Sudden Change | Immediate Action
Accident | Quick Decision | Severance
Swift Resolution | Breaking Free

The Scythe card is all about cutting through the noise and making quick decisions. This card is like a wake-up call, urging you to take action. It often points to a situation where you can't just sit back and wait. Whether it's resolving a problem, confronting a truth, or making a clean break, sometimes you need to be decisive to clear the path ahead.

This card also has a strong association with something ending. It might be time to let go of things that are holding you back—a relationship, a job, or even a habit. It encourages you to face uncomfortable truths and cut ties that no longer serve you. While endings can be difficult, they're often necessary so space can be created for something better to come.

The Scythe is a powerful reminder to act decisively. It tells you that while cutting things out of your life can be challenging, it's also a chance for transformation and renewal. So, when you see the Scythe, take a deep breath and get ready to tackle whatever it is that needs your attention. Change might be uncomfortable, but it can lead to a brighter path ahead.

11 Whip

Conflict | Negative Patterns
Tension | Confrontation | Training
Repetition | Drive | Discipline

11 Whip

> Conflict | Negative Patterns
> Tension | Confrontation | Training
> Repetition | Drive | Discipline

When you see the Whip card, it usually indicates some sort of struggle or disagreement, whether it's in a relationship, work, or even within yourself. It might suggest that there's some unresolved issue that needs to be addressed. Rather than sweeping things under the rug, confront those challenges head-on.

The Whip card often points to a struggle with repetition and patterns. It might be highlighting those patterns you keep repeating, whether in relationships, habits, or situations. You know those times when you find yourself stuck in the same argument with a friend or falling into the same old routine? It's time to break free from those cycles so you can create a more positive path forward.

Ultimately, the Whip is about recognizing the power of confrontation and the potential for transformation that comes from facing difficult situations. Don't shy away from uncomfortable conversations or situations; they can lead to growth and clarity. So when you see the Whip, consider it a call to take action, address conflicts, and harness that energy for positive change.

12 Birds

Chatter | Gossip | Excitement
Communication | Stress | Anxiety
Socializing | Conversation

12 Birds

**Chatter | Gossip | Excitement
Communication | Stress | Anxiety
Socializing | Conversation**

When you see this card, it's a sign that conversations, discussions, or even gossip may be playing a big role in your situation. Whether it's chatting with friends, engaging in meetings, or exchanging important information, the Birds represent the flow of communication and the buzz of social connections. This card can be a reminder to pay attention to the conversations happening around you.

On the flip side, the Birds can also point to nervous energy or stress. You might feel a bit scattered or anxious, especially if there's a lot of talk going on without much action. It's that feeling of being overwhelmed by all the chatter—whether it's in your own head or from others. Focus on what's important, and avoid getting too caught up in gossip or trivial discussions that drain your energy.

In general, the Birds card highlights communication, both positive and negative. Be mindful of the messages you're sending and receiving, and navigate social interactions with care. Whether it's a light conversation or a serious discussion, always stay present and clear in your communication.

13 Child

Innocence | Playfulness | Trust
Naivety | Fresh Start | Small Steps
Curiosity | Learning | Simplicity

13 Child

> Innocence | Playfulness | Trust
> Naivety | Fresh Start | Small Steps
> Curiosity | Learning | Simplicity

The Child card is all about new beginnings, innocence, and fresh perspectives. It's often a sign that you're entering a phase where you can approach things with a sense of curiosity and wonder, just as a child would. Whether it's a new project, relationship, or chapter in life, embrace simplicity and take things one step at a time. It's not about rushing forward but enjoying the process of discovery along the way.

This card also speaks to youthfulness and playfulness. Let go of overcomplications or heavy burdens and to approach situations with a lighter heart. Feel the sense of joy and exploration that invites you to look at the world through fresh eyes and see opportunities for growth that you might not have noticed before. It's about being open to learning and embracing new experiences.

At the same time, the Child can also highlight naivety or inexperience. While there's beauty in being open and curious, the card can remind you to be mindful being too trusting or overlooking important details. The Child card ultimately encourages you to stay grounded as you nurture a sense of wonder.

14 Fox

Deception | Cunning | Trickery
Strategy | Craftiness | Adaptability
Observant | Self-Reliant

14 Fox

> Deception | Cunning | Trickery
> Strategy | Craftiness | Adaptability
> Observant | Self-Reliant

When the Fox card appears, it signals that you need to be clever and strategic in your approach. Don't jump into situations blindly; instead, take a step back, analyze your circumstances, and find a smart, calculated way forward. Whether in relationships, work, or personal challenges, this card reminds you to rely on your instincts and use your wits to navigate any tricky situations.

On the flip side, the Fox can also carry a warning about deceit or manipulation. It may indicate that someone in your environment is being less than honest or acting with hidden motives. Keep your eyes open for potential trickery, and trust your gut if something feels off. Be discerning about who you trust and mindful of any deals or offers that seem too good to be true.

In essence, the Fox is about being sharp and adaptable. It's not necessarily negative, but it asks you to think strategically and protect your interests. Whether it's avoiding pitfalls or finding clever solutions, be smart, stay alert, and trust your own ability to handle challenges with skill and precision.

15 Bear

Strength | Power | Authority
Dominance | Influence | Intimidation
Control | Confidence | Leadership

15 Bear

> Strength | Power | Authority
> Dominance | Influence | Intimidation
> Control | Confidence | Leadership

The Bear card indicates someone or something in a position of influence or control. This could be a protective figure in your life, such as a mentor, boss, or parental figure, or it could point to your own ability to assert dominance in a situation. The Bear is all about leadership, protection, and the use of power, whether it's to support others or to stand strong on your own.

The Bear is a card of authority, but with authority comes responsibility. If you're facing a situation that requires you to step up, take control with confidence. On the flip side, take care that you're not overbearing and that you don't use your power in a way that could intimidate or overwhelm others.

In financial or career matters, the Bear often signifies financial security or stability, sometimes through someone who is well-established or experienced. Decisions made now can have a lasting impact. Whether you're the one wielding the power or relying on someone else's strength, remain wise, steady, and grounded in your approach.

16 Stars

Hope | Inspiration | Guidance
Spirituality | Insight | Aspirations
Enlightenment | Vision | Dreams

16 Stars

> Hope | Inspiration | Guidance
> Spirituality | Insight | Aspirations
> Enlightenment | Vision | Dreams

When the Stars card appears, it brings a sense of optimism and clarity, like a bright star shining in the night sky to help you navigate through life's uncertainties. Look to your dreams and aspirations,. You're on the right path, even if things feel unclear at the moment. Keep your goals in sight and trust in the direction you're headed.

The card also represents guidance, often suggesting that help or advice is available to you. Whether it's through your intuition, external signs, or someone offering wisdom, the Stars point toward finding your way with clarity and purpose. Stay aligned with your higher self and to trust in the larger picture, even when you can't see every step ahead.

In a broader sense, the Stars indicate inspiration and spiritual insight. You may experience a time of enlightenment or a moment where things suddenly become clear, allowing you to move forward with confidence. Whether in your personal, professional, or spiritual life, embrace your potential and aim high, knowing you're supported by the universe.

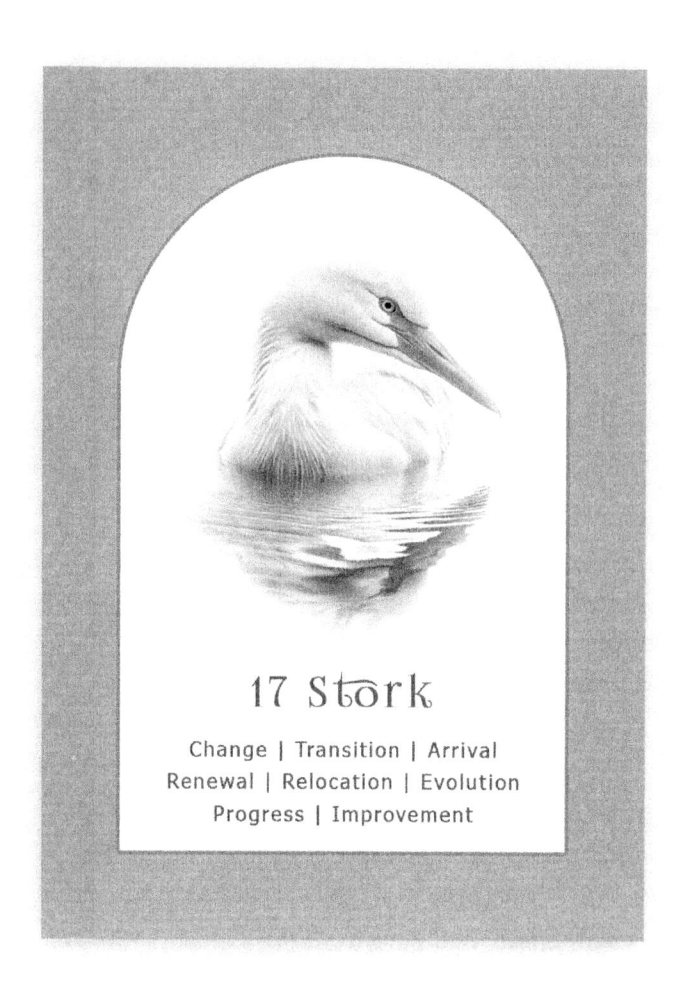

17 Stork

Change | Transition | Arrival
Renewal | Relocation | Evolution
Progress | Improvement

17 Stork

Change | Transition | Arrival
Renewal | Relocation | Evolution
Progress | Improvement

The Stork card suggests that something in your life is shifting, often bringing new beginnings or a positive transition. Just as the stork is known for delivering new life, this card hints at a fresh start or a significant improvement in a current situation. You may soon find yourself in a new environment, mindset, or phase of life.

The Stork also speaks to personal growth and development. Whether it's a new job, relationship, or lifestyle change, it's likely to bring about something beneficial. It's a card of progress, telling you to move forward with an open heart and a readiness to adapt to what's coming.

In addition, the Stork can highlight the arrival of news or developments that shift your perspective. It often signifies that the change is already in motion, whether or not you're fully aware of it yet. Go with the flow, trust the process, and know that the changes happening are aligned with your personal growth and future success.

18 Dog

Loyalty | Friendship | Support
Devotion | Faithfulness | Reliability
Allies | Trust | Connection

18 Dog

**Loyalty | Friendship | Support
Devotion | Faithfulness | Reliability
Allies | Trust | Connection**

The Dog card is a symbol of loyalty, friendship, and companionship. It emphasizes strong bonds with others and the importance of trust and support in your relationships. Appreciate the loyal people in your life—those who stand by you through thick and thin. It's a reminder that you're not alone. You have allies who genuinely care about your well-being.

This card also represents faithfulness and devotion, both in friendships and in romantic relationships. If you're navigating a situation where loyalty is called into question, true friendships will withstand the test of time. Nurture those connections and recognizing the value of having someone you can rely on.

On a broader scale, the Dog signifies a need for companionship or community. If you're feeling isolated or alone, this card encourages you to reach out and build connections with others. Whether through socializing, joining groups, or simply leaning on friends, fostering these relationships can bring much-needed support into your life.

19 Tower

Authority | Boundaries | Isolation
Structure | Bureaucracy | Government
Institutions | Systems | Rules

19 Tower

> Authority | Boundaries | Isolation
> Structure | Bureaucracy | Government
> Institutions | Systems | Rules

The Tower card often represents organizations, institutions, or systems that provide a sense of order and control. It can suggest that you're dealing with something large and established, like a big company, the government, or some kind of formal structure in your life. It's about setting boundaries, maintaining discipline, and keeping things organized.

On a more personal level, the Tower can symbolize independence or even isolation. You might be feeling a little distant or detached, standing alone to gain perspective or protect yourself. While independence is important, avoid becoming too rigid or cut off from others. There's a fine balance between self-sufficiency and shutting out other people.

At times, the Tower can also hint at control issues or the negative side of authority, such as feeling trapped by bureaucracy or overwhelmed by power structures. Be mindful of how much control you exert—or allow others to exert—over your life.

20 Garden

Networking | Events | Society
Socializing | Community | Gathering
Collaboration | Shared Interests

20 Garden

**Networking | Events | Society
Socializing | Community | Gathering
Collaboration | Shared Interests**

The Garden card represents social interactions, community, public spaces, or other opportunities where people come together. This is a time for socializing, networking, or participating in group activities. The Garden is about connections—whether it's with friends, family, colleagues, or even strangers—and highlights the importance of engaging with others.

On a deeper level, the Garden can symbolize the public or the collective. It represents not only physical places where people meet but also the broader idea of being seen and interacting in public forums, both online and offline. The key to your situation lies in making the right connections with the people around you.

This card encourages you to be receptive and collaborative. Success may come through teamwork, attending events, or networking with others. The Garden is a reminder to nurture your social relationships and embrace opportunities to expand your circle, as these connections could bring new growth and possibilities into your life.

21 Mountain

Obstacles | Challenge | Struggle
Detour | Frustration | Stagnation
Resistance | Delay | Hardship

21 Mountain

> Obstacle | Challenge | Struggle
> Detour | Frustration | Stagnation
> Resistance | Delay | Hardship

The Mountain card represents challenges, delays, or obstacles. It symbolizes the things that stand in your way and make progress slower or more difficult. This card often appears when you're facing a significant hurdle, whether it's a problem that needs solving, a delay in plans, or something blocking your path.

When the Mountain shows up, it's not necessarily saying that success is out of reach—it's just further away than expected. It's like a tough climb that demands extra effort, resilience, and determination. While the journey might be harder than you'd hoped, the rewards at the top can still be worthwhile if you're willing to push through the rough terrain.

The Mountain can also represent feelings of frustration or stagnation, where progress seems to be at a standstill. Now is the time to recognize what's holding you back and to take a strategic approach to overcome the challenge. Whether it's a situation you need to navigate around or a problem you have to tackle head-on, perseverance is key.

22 Path

Free Will | Alternatives
Choice | Decision Point | Options
Uncertainty | Turning Point

22 Path

> Free Will | Alternatives
> Choice | Decision Point | Options
> Uncertainty | Turning Point

The Path card is all about choices, decisions, and new directions. It signifies those moments in life when you stand at a fork in the road, and you need to decide which way to go. This card often appears when it's time to weigh your options carefully, signaling that a choice you make now will have a lasting impact on your future.

When the Path appears, it highlights the importance of trusting your instincts and using your judgment to make the right decision. Consider each option carefully and think about where each path might lead before committing to a direction.

This card can also reflect feelings of indecision or being at a crossroads in life where it's difficult to pick a direction. It suggests that while it might feel overwhelming, don't be afraid to take that first step. Now is the time to take control of your journey, make decisions with confidence, and know that whatever road you choose, it will lead you in the direction you're supposed to go.

23 Mice

Slow Decay | Loss | Theft
Gradual Decline | Deterioration
Erosion | Nuisance | Depletion

23 Mice

> Slow Decay | Loss | Theft
> Gradual Decline | Deterioration
> Erosion | Nuisance | Depletion

The Mice card represents loss, stress, and gradual decay. It points to the small but persistent problems that slowly drain energy, resources, or time, often without you noticing right away. Pay attention to what's quietly eating away at your peace of mind or the things you value.

When the Mice card shows up, it's a sign that something may be eroding your sense of stability or comfort. This could manifest as stress, worry, or feelings of anxiety that slowly build up until they become overwhelming. Something tangible may be slipping away—like your finances, or your sense of security. Identify what's causing this "slow leak" in your life and take action before it becomes a bigger problem.

This card doesn't necessarily signal a major disaster. It emphasizes the importance of being aware of the little things that can add up. By addressing the minor issues now—whether it's stress, nagging worries, or small financial setbacks—you can prevent them from becoming major obstacles.

24 Heart

Love | Affection | Romance
Compassion | Intimacy | Passion
Emotional Connection

24 Heart

**Love | Affection | Romance
Compassion | Intimacy | Passion
Emotional Connection**

The Heart card represents love, affection, and emotional connections. It's all about those warm, fuzzy feelings that come from deep relationships, whether romantic, familial, or friendly. When this card appears, it signals a strong bond with someone in your life. It invites you to embrace joy, compassion, intimacy, and the importance of nurturing your relationships.

The Heart card suggests that love is in the air or that you should focus on the relationships that bring you happiness. Express your feelings, show kindness, and be open to receiving love from others. You may experience new romantic beginnings or a deepening of existing connections, reminding you that love often requires attention and care to flourish.

The Heart card encourages you to prioritize emotional well-being. Happiness often comes from the connections you build with others. Whether it's through simple acts of kindness or meaningful conversations, the Heart card emphasizes the value of creating and maintaining bonds that bring you joy.

25 Ring

Connection | Promise | Fidelity
Commitment | Partnership | Alliance
Relationship | Agreement | Union

25 Ring

**Connection | Promise | Fidelity
Commitment | Partnership | Alliance
Relationship | Agreement | Union**

The Ring card symbolizes commitments, partnerships, and cycles. It's often associated with promises and contracts, making it a powerful card in readings about relationships and agreements. It indicates that a significant bond is forming or already exists, whether it's romantic, business-related, or about a close friendship.

The Ring card suggests a deepening connection or a commitment that may be on the horizon. This could manifest as engagements, marriages, or other forms of dedication that signify a strong partnership. If you're in a situation that requires negotiation or collaboration, you have the potential for mutually beneficial agreements.

The Ring card is also about the cyclical nature of life. It reminds you that what goes around comes around, highlighting the importance of the choices you make and the commitments you uphold. Reflect on the patterns in your life and embrace positive cycles at the same time you address those that may need to change.

26 Book

Hidden Information | Curiosity
Knowledge | Secrets | Mystery
Education | Revelation

26 Book

> Hidden Information | Curiosity
> Knowledge | Secrets | Mystery
> Education | Revelation

The Book card represents knowledge, secrets, and hidden information. It signifies the quest for understanding and the process of learning, whether through formal education or personal exploration. It's possible that not everything in your current situation is transparent, suggesting that undisclosed truths or mysteries may need to be unraveled.

Now is the time to embrace curiosity and be open to acquiring new knowledge. Expanding your understanding can lead to personal development and enlightenment. This could mean pursuing formal education, taking up a new hobby, or simply seeking experiences that broaden your horizons.

On a more introspective level, the Book also invites you to reflect on your own secrets and inner truths. It may be a sign to examine aspects of yourself that you keep hidden, encouraging honesty and self-discovery. Whether it's about uncovering secrets or delving into your inner thoughts, knowledge is key to navigating your journey.

27 Letter

Announcement | Document
Written Word | Delivery | Contract
Correspondence | Paperwork

27 Letter

**Announcement | Document
Written Word | Delivery | Contract
Correspondence | Paperwork**

The Letter card embodies communication, messages, and information exchange. You may receive important news or correspondence that could impact your situation. This could be a letter, an email, a text, or any form of written communication. The Letter card emphasizes the importance of clarity and understanding, reminding you to pay attention to the details in messages you receive.

In addition to indicating news, the Letter card can also signify the expression of thoughts and feelings. It encourages you to communicate your own messages clearly and openly, whether that's sharing your emotions with someone or drafting an important document.

The Letter card may highlight the significance of formal documentation and contracts. Agreements or commitments may be on the horizon, so read the fine print and ensure you're clear on the terms. Effective communication is key to navigating relationships and situations successfully and can lead to greater clarity and insight.

28 Man

Masculine Presence | Male Energy
Significant Other | Logic | Directness
Action-Oriented | Focused Energy

28 Man

**Masculine Presence | Male Energy
Significant Other | Logic | Directness
Action-Oriented | Focused Energy**

The Man card represents a significant masculine figure or you if you are male. This card is straightforward in its focus—it's all about a particular male presence in a situation. It doesn't carry any inherent positive or negative connotations; its meaning depends on the surrounding cards and the context of the reading.

In readings about relationships, the Man card often symbolizes a partner, love interest, or someone with a major impact on your life. If it shows up alongside cards that suggest emotion, like the Heart, it can point to love and affection. Conversely, if it appears with cards like the Snake or Whip, it might signal conflict, deception, or challenges connected to this person.

For career or life path questions, the Man card can refer to a male colleague, mentor, or authority figure who plays a pivotal role. The Man card encourages taking initiative, being direct, and understanding the influence this masculine energy has on the issue at hand.

29 Woman

Female Presence | Female Energy
Significant Other | Intuition | Empathy
Emotional Depth | Sensitivity

29 Woman

> **Feminine Presence | Female Energy**
> **Significant Other | Intuition | Empathy**
> **Emotional Depth | Sensitivity**

The Woman card represents a key feminine presence in your life or situation. When this card appears, it typically points to a woman who holds importance in the context of your question—this could be a partner, friend, colleague, or even you, if you are female. The card draws attention to themes like nurturing, intuition, and emotional insight, highlighting how these qualities play a role in your current situation.

This card brings a focus on empathy, understanding, and the softer, more reflective side of matters. It suggests that now might be the time to tune in to your feelings or the emotions of those around you. The Woman card encourages you to consider how sensitivity and a more open approach could help in navigating challenges or relationships.

The Woman card indicates the influence of a female partner or the emotional dynamics between you and someone else. It can point to the power of intuition, suggesting a more empathetic or thoughtful approach.

30 Lily

Wisdom | Maturity | Peace
Integrity | Serenity | Virtue | Ethics
Purity | Tranquility | Experience

30 Lily

**Wisdom | Maturity | Peace
Integrity | Serenity | Virtue | Ethics
Purity | Tranquility | Experience**

The Lily card symbolizes peace, maturity, and a sense of calm that comes from experience. When this card shows up, it suggests that the situation you're dealing with might benefit from a steady, thoughtful approach. This is a time of reflection or a need to slow down and appreciate the wisdom that comes with time and patience.

The Lily card touches on themes of wisdom, integrity, and virtue. Acting with a sense of morality and staying true to your core values will serve you well in your current situation. Whether it's a personal dilemma or a professional challenge, lean on your past experiences and approach things with a sense of grace. If there are conflicts, maintaining composure and aiming for harmony will yield the best results.

The Lily can indicate a connection that's based on trust, stability, and mutual respect. It suggests a bond that's been built over time, or that's in need of a more mature and understanding perspective. Overall, the Lily card is about embracing the value of patience, wisdom, and a gentle touch.

31 Sun

Positive Energy | Success | Victory
Optimism | Achievement | Confidence
Radiance | Triumph | Impact

31 Sun

Positivity Energy | Success | Victory
Optimism | Achievement | Confidence
Radiance | Triumph | Impact

The Sun card is a powerful symbol of positivity and success. It's like getting a burst of sunlight in your reading, signaling joy, happiness, and a sense of fulfillment. It represents a time when things are going well for you, and you might find that your efforts are finally paying off. You'll feel more energized, ready to tackle challenges with a bright outlook.

In relationships, the Sun signifies joy and harmony. It suggests that your connections will flourish, bringing happiness and mutual understanding. Celebrate your bonds with loved ones and to be open to new friendships. The Sun's warmth can help dispel any misunderstandings, fostering a better sense of trust and support among those around you.

When it comes to work, the Sun indicates a period of achievement and recognition. Your hard work is likely to pay off, leading to success and possibly even public acknowledgment. Stay optimistic and keep pushing forward. Trust in your abilities, and don't hesitate to take center stage when the opportunity arises.

32 Moon

Emotions | Intuition | Dreams
Creativity | Imagination | Cycles
Subconscious | Hidden Truth

32 Moon

**Emotions | Intuition | Dreams
Creativity | Imagination | Cycles
Subconscious | Hidden Truth**

The Moon card represents intuition, emotions, and the unseen aspects of life. This is a time to tune into your inner self and pay attention to your feelings. Trust your instincts and explore your dreams, as they often symbolizes the deeper currents that shape your thoughts and actions.

In relationships, the Moon indicates emotional depth and sensitivity. It can signify a time of heightened feelings, where you may find yourself more attuned to the emotions of those around you. This card invites you to embrace vulnerability and open up about your feelings, fostering closer connections. However, it also warns of potential misunderstandings or illusions, so be honest with yourself and your partner.

When it comes to work or creative endeavors, the Moon encourages you to explore your imagination and intuition. However, be mindful of any uncertainties or lack of clarity in your work environment. The Moon advises you to look beyond the surface and consider the underlying dynamics at play

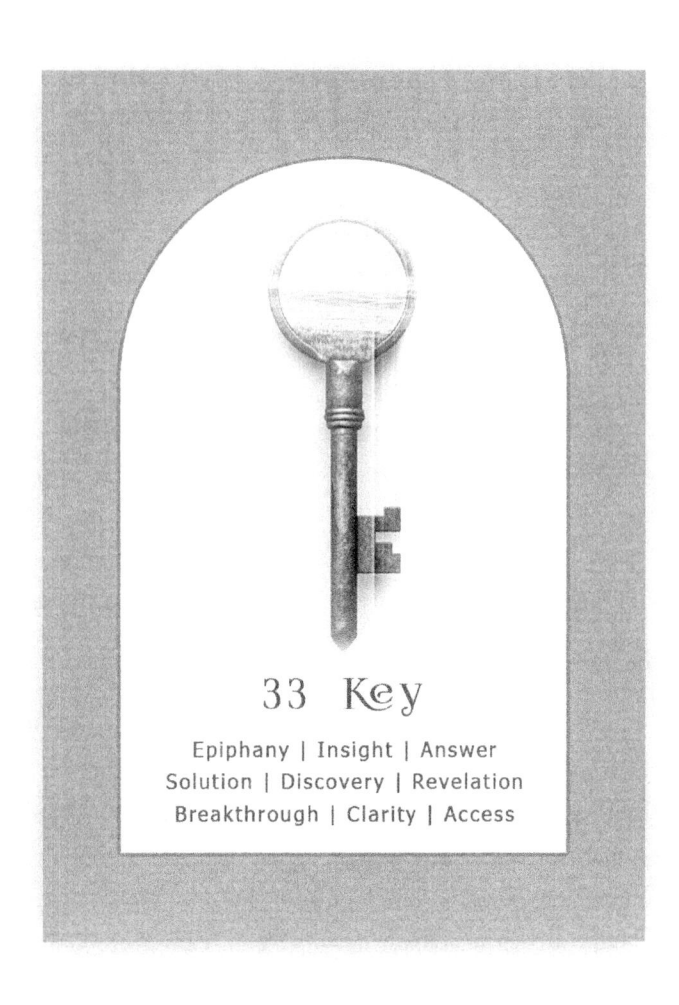

33 Key

Epiphany | Insight | Answer
Solution | Discovery | Revelation
Breakthrough | Clarity | Access

33 Key

> Epiphany | Insight | Answer
> Solution | Discovery | Revelation
> Breakthrough | Clarity | Access

The Key card is a powerful indication that you hold the answers to the challenges you're facing. Trust your intuition and knowledge, as they will guide you toward resolving issues and making significant progress.

In relationships, the Key signifies the potential for deeper understanding and connection. It may point to important conversations or revelations that can strengthen your bond with others. If you're facing obstacles, finding common ground or opening up about your feelings can lead to breakthroughs.

When it comes to work or personal goals, the Key represents significant opportunities for advancement. It suggests that your hard work is about to pay off, and new doors are opening for you. This card invites you to be proactive in pursuing your ambitions, as success is just a step away. Trust your instincts, and don't hesitate to seize opportunities as they arise, for the Key signifies that you are on the path to achieving your goals and aspirations.

34 Fish

Wealth | Business | Finances
Resources | Self-Reliance | Flow
Abundance | Prosperity

34 Fish

**Wealth | Business | Finances
Resources | Self-Reliance | Flow
Abundance | Prosperity**

The Fish card represents abundance, wealth, and the flow of resources. It signals opportunities to enhance your financial situation or expand your personal and professional horizons. Think about how you manage your resources, realizing that prosperity arises from the right balance between effort and flow.

In your work or business, the Fish points to success and expansion. You might be entering a period of growth where your investments—whether financial, emotional, or creative—are paying off. You have a potential for profit, but remember to stay adaptable and follow the currents of opportunity when they appear.

On a personal level, the Fish card can also reflect emotional or spiritual abundance. Explore what truly makes you feel rich and fulfilled. Whether it's relationships, creative projects, or simply the joy of living, cherish and nurture the things that bring depth and flow to your life. Embrace the sense of ease and generosity the Fish offers, knowing that abundance comes in many forms.

35 Anchor

Hard Work | Dependability
Grounding | Reliability | Resilience
Long-Term Success | Foundation

35 Anchor

> Hard Work | Dependability
> Grounding | Reliability | Resilience
> Long-Term Success | Foundation

The Anchor card represents stability, security, and persistence. It's a reminder to stay grounded and focused on your goals. It encourages you to build a strong foundation, whether in your career, relationships, or personal lfe. The Anchor signals that success comes from consistent effort and determination.

In your professional life, the Anchor suggests long-term commitment and reliability. It may point to a steady job, a dependable routine, or the need to establish firm boundaries to ensure your stability. If things feel uncertain, this card reassures you that persistence will eventually secure the outcome you're aiming for.

On a personal level, the Anchor can also symbolize emotional security and a sense of belonging. Reflect on the things or people that ground you. However, it's important to watch out for stagnation; while the Anchor provides stability, it can also hold you back if you cling to something out of fear of change.

36 Cross

Burden | Responsibility | Faith
Obligation | Suffering | Spirituality
Redemption | Moral Lesson

36 Cross

**Burden | Responsibility | Faith
Obligation | Suffering | Spirituality
Redemption | Moral Lesson**

The Cross card is a powerful symbol of burdens, responsibilities, and spiritual lessons. It often points to something you're carrying—a responsibility, hardship, or moral obligation—that feels heavy or unavoidable. It's a reminder that while struggles are part of life, they can also be meaningful opportunities for growth and resilience.

In your daily life, the Cross might highlight a situation where you feel overwhelmed. Recognize the weight you're bearing and consider whether it's something you need to endure or if it's time to let go. This card can point to a sense of duty or faith, calling you to confront your challenges with courage.

Emotionally, the Cross can bring attention to pain, grief, or sacrifice. It invites you to process these feelings, not as a punishment, but as a part of your journey. This card asks you to have compassion for yourself as you navigate difficult times. Ultimately, the Cross is a card of acceptance, of learning to embrace both the struggles and the lessons they bring.

BASICS OF LENORMAND READING

Reading Lenormand cards involves interpreting a compact, symbolic language to gain insights into various aspects of life. Unlike Tarot, which focuses on spiritual and pyschological realms, Lenormand is straightforward and practical, focusing on concrete situations and events.

PRACTICAL AND DIRECT INSIGHTS
Lenormand readings provide clear, practical answers. Each card has a specific and often literal meaning, such as news (Rider), luck (Clover), or travel (Ship). The cards collectively describe events, people, and situations with a focus on tangible outcomes rather than abstract concepts.

COMBINING CARD MEANINGS
The core of Lenormand reading lies in combining card meanings. Rather than focusing on individual cards in isolation, Lenormand emphasizes the interaction between cards. This interaction is often read in pairs, lines, or larger spreads, creating a narrative that describes the situation in question.

SIMPLE SYMBOLISM
The cards in a Lenormand deck each feature clear symbols, such as animals, objects, or natural elements. These symbols represent everyday concepts and are designed to be easily recognizable, making the system accessible and intuitive.

CONTEXT AND POSITION
The meaning of each card can shift based on its context within a spread and its position relative to other cards. For example, a card representing difficulty might imply different things if it appears next to a card symbolizing love versus a card about career.

FIXED AND PREDICTIVE NATURE
Lenormand is often used for predictive readings. It excels in forecasting specific outcomes, making it ideal for questions about future events, decisions, and short-term planning. Its interpretations are often more fixed and less subject to personal development themes than Tarot.

FOCUS ON DAILY LIFE
Lenormand readings are well-suited for addressing everyday issues and decisions. They often deal with practical matters like relationships, career, finances, and health, offering guidance on immediate concerns.

DAILY DRAWS
Many readers start with a daily card draw, pulling one or two cards to gain insight into the day's events. This helps in understanding how card meanings play out in real life.

LAYOUTS AND SPREADS
Lenormand readings can range from simple one-or two-card draws to more complex spreads. The layout depends on the complexity of the question and the depth of insight needed. Some examples include the following:

3-Card Spread: A common method to read a three-card spread is to read cards 1 and 2 together, then cards 2 and 3, and then combine those meanings into a cohesive summary.

9-Card Spread: Provides a broader perspective on a situation. Cards are read in three-card groupings, vertically, horizontally and diagonally.

Grand Tableau: Uses all the cards in the deck and provides an indepth view of the querent's life.

While Lenormand is more structured, intuition still plays a role. Experienced readers blend traditional meanings with their intuitive insights to provide a well-rounded interpretation.

Lenormand card reading is a practical and accessible method of divination that offers direct answers to everyday questions. By combining straightforward symbols with various interpretative techniques, it provides clarity and guidance on specific life situations, making it a valuable tool for those seeking concrete advice and predictions.

READING CARD PAIRS

To read Lenormand card pairs, you combine the meanings of two cards to produce a cohesive interpretation.

SEQUENTIAL READING: The cards are read in order.

    Clover + House = Something fortunate at home
    House + Clover = Your home environment brings luck

    Snake + Garden = Complications in a social setting
    Garden + Snake = A social event causes complications

    Child + Key = A new beginning that brings opportunity
    Key + Child = An opportunity for a new beginning

    Book + Star = Knowledge leads to guidance
    Star + Book = Guided to a source of knowledge

    Bouquet + Cross = Finding joy in hardship
    Cross + Bouquet = Hardship that leads to joy

MODIFIER APPROACH: The first card acts as the noun, and the second card modifies it, providing more context or detail.

    Rider + Mountain = Delayed news or message
    Letter + Sun = Positive email or a successful contract
    Birds + Anchor = Supportive conversation

Ring + Clover = Short agreement or fun partnership
Cross + Tree = Long-term burden or deep faith
Snake + Scythe = Sudden difficulty or end to betrayal

TIPS FOR EFFECTIVE PAIR READING

Consider Contextual Variations: If you draw the Clover + House, and the reading pertains to relationships, it could imply a joyful domestic relationship. If it's about finances, it might suggest a lucky financial opportunity tied to real estate or family resources.

Trust Your Intuition: While foundational meanings are essential, your intuition can provide additional insights.

Practice Regularly: Use daily draws or small spreads to practice pair readings.

CARDS WITH SIMILARITIES

RIDER AND SCYTHE

The **Rider** and **Scythe** cards both signal swift action and change, but they do so in different ways.

The **Rider** represents news, messages, or opportunities that arrive quickly. It often brings new developments or updates. This card symbolizes the arrival of something, whether it's a person, an idea, or a piece of news, and signals forward momentum.

The **Scythe** represents swift action that results in cutting away or decisive decisions. It can indicate a sudden change, such as an abrupt ending, removal, or sharp action taken to clear the way. This card can sometimes bring a sense of danger or harm due to its quick, cutting nature.

> The **Rider** card focuses on arrival and movement, bringing news or opportunities. It is about forward progress or something coming toward you.
>
> The **Scythe** card focuses on sudden, sharp action or an abrupt ending. It is about a sharp removal or cutting of something away from your life.

HEART AND RING

The **Heart** and **Ring** cards both relate to relationships, but they focus on different aspects of connection and commitment.

The **Heart** card represents love, emotions, and passion. It focuses on the feelings, affection, and emotional bonds within a relationship, particularly romantic or heartfelt connections. It is about the emotional experience of love and compassion.

The **Ring** card represents commitments and contracts. It focuses on agreements, promises, and enduring bonds, whether in romantic relationships, business partnerships, or other formal arrangements.

> The **Heart** card focuses on emotional bonds. It is about romance or passion within a relationship.
>
> The **Ring** card focuses on the formal or binding nature of a connection or promise. It is about commitments and agreements within a relationship.

HOUSE AND TREE

The **House** and **Tree** cards both deal with stability and foundational aspects of life, but they focus on different domains.

The **House** card represents home, family, and personal security. It focuses on domestic life, physical spaces, and the comfort and stability of one's personal environment. It emphasizes belonging, protection, and a structured foundation.

The **Tree** card represents health, growth, and life's roots. It focuses on long-term well-being, personal development, and the strength from feeling connected to to ancestry or spirituality.

> The **House** card focuses on security in a domestic or familial sense. It is about a place of comfort and safety.
>
> The **Tree** card focuses on physical health, growth, and the organic progression of life. It is about life's interconnectedness and the strength that comes from deep roots.

COFFIN AND STORK

The **Coffin** and **Stork** cards both signify transformation, but they emphasize different aspects of change.

The **Coffin** represents endings, closure, and the need to let go. It signifies a period of transition that often involves loss, rest, or finality. The Coffin is about completion and the emotional or practical adjustments that come with an ending.

The **Stork** represents change, renewal, and movement forward. It focuses on new beginnings, transformations, or relocations, often associated with progress and positive shifts. The Stork is about embracing growth and moving toward something new.

> The **Coffin** card focuses on endings or the conclusion of a chapter in your life. It is about loss, completion, or finality.
>
> The **Stork** card focuses on new beginnings and transitions into something better. It is about progress, opportunity, and forward-looking optimism.

SNAKE AND FOX

The **Snake** and **Fox** cards share themes of cunning and deception, but they differ in their underlying nature, intent, and specific contexts.

The **Snake** is usually focused on relational dynamics, such as jealousy, betrayal, or seduction. This card often involves calculated manipulation, often for personal gain or emotional influence.

The **Fox** is focused on self-reliance, strategic thinking, or situations requiring sharp instincts. This card involves using cunning or resourcefulness to survive or thrive, often with a selfish undertone, with the goal of protecting personal interests.

> The **Snake** card focuses on using cunning and deceit to inflict harm and achieve personal gain. It is about complex, underhanded, and potentially treacherous behavior.
>
> The **Fox** card focuses on using cunning and deceit as a strategy for self-protection. It is about wary, cautious and distrustful behavior.

BOUQUET AND SUN

The **Bouquet** and **Sun** cards both convey warm, positive energy, but their focus and nature differ.

The **Bouquet** represents gifts, gratitude, and charm. It focuses on moments of appreciation, beauty, and the small joys of life, often symbolizing social harmony or receiving a pleasant surprise. The Bouquet is about kind gestures, compliments, and enjoying life's pleasures.

The **Sun** represents success, vitality, and confidence. It focuses on personal achievement, clarity, and the power to overcome challenges. The Sun radiates energy and optimism, bringing a sense of empowerment and illumination.

> The **Bouquet** card focuses on beauty, gratitude, and moments of joy and happiness, often involving interactions with others. It is about enjoying life's pleasures.
>
> The **Sun** card focuses on personal success, energy, and achievement. It is about confidence, personal success, and big-picture accomplishments.

BIRDS AND LETTER

The **Birds** and **Letter** cards both deal with communication, but they focus on different types and contexts.

The **Birds** card represents conversation, chatter, and verbal exchanges. It highlights discussions, gossip, phone calls, or any dynamic, back-and-forth communication. Birds often involve social interaction or situations where words are exchanged in real-time.

The **Letter** card represents written communication, documents, or messages. It focuses on formal, tangible forms of communication, such as letters, emails, or contracts. The Letter emphasizes information being delivered in a static, structured way.

> The **Birds** card focuses on spoken or dynamic communication, often conversational or informal. It is about the real-time exhange of ideas or participation in dialogue.
>
> The **Letter** card focuses on delivering or receiving a clear, tangible message. It is about written or formal communication.

DOG AND HEART

The **Dog** and **Heart** cards in both relate to relationships, but they emphasize different aspects.

The **Dog** represents friendship, trustworthiness, and loyalty. It focuses on supportive, dependable relationships, particularly platonic or collaborative ones. The **Dog** signifies faithful companionship and mutual reliability.

The **Heart** represents love, passion, and emotions. It focuses on matters of the heart, including romantic love, emotional connections, and feelings of affection. The Heart emphasizes emotional bonds and intimacy.

> The **Dog** card focuses on loyalty and trust, often within platonic or supportive relationships. It is about being a steady, reliable presence.
>
> The **Heart** card focuses on love and romantic feelings. It is about emotional depth and passion.

SAMPLE TWO-CARD READINGS

FISH + ANCHOR

34 Fish
Wealth | Business | Finances
Resources | Self-Reliance | Flow
Abundance | Prosperity

35 Anchor
Hard Work | Dependability
Grounding | Reliability | Resilience
Long-Term Success | Foundation

Together, the Fish and Anchor cards suggest that improving your financial position (Fish) will require focusing on building lasting stability and securing a solid foundation (Anchor).

How does my boyfriend feel about marriage? He likely views marriage as a means of creating lasting stability and security (Anchor), with an emphasis on emotional and material prosperity (Fish). He seems to value commitment and may see marriage as a solid, dependable foundation for both emotional fulfillment and future growth.

What should I do to improve my financial situation? Focus on creating a steady, long-term plan (Anchor) that fosters growth and stability (Fish). Look for opportunities to increase your financial security by making smart, sustainable investments or building a solid career foundation that ensures consistent income and wealth over time.

SNAKE + MICE

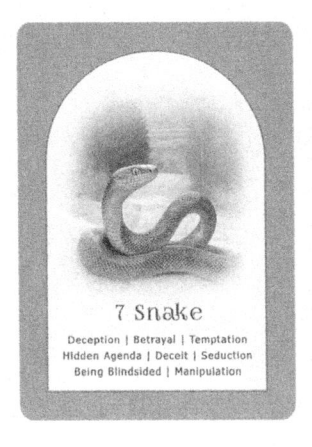

7 Snake
Deception | Betrayal | Temptation
Hidden Agenda | Deceit | Seduction
Being Blindsided | Manipulation

23 Mice
Slow Decay | Loss | Theft
Gradual Decline | Deterioration
Erosion | Nuisance | Depletion

Together, the Snake and Mice cards suggest issues related to hidden tensions or financial/emotional losses (Mice) caused by deceit or a hidden agenda (Snake).

What should I look for in a potential partner? Be cautious of someone who may bring hidden problems or deceit (Snake) that could cause ongoing stress or loss (Mice). Look for a partner who is open, honest, and able to address issues directly without causing emotional turmoil.

How can I get along better with my teenage son? To improve your relationship, address any underlying tensions or problems that may be causing stress or small conflicts (Mice). Be mindful of potential hidden issues (Snake), and work together to clear misunderstandings or negative patterns that might be undermining your connection.

BEAR + COFFIN

15 Bear
Strength | Power | Authority
Dominance | Influence | Intimidation
Control | Confidence | Leadership

8 Coffin
Endings | Loss | Grief
Transition | Release of the Past
Letting Go | Transformation

Together, the Bear and Coffin cards indicate the end of a phase (Coffin) where you felt secure or in control (Bear), possibly tied to a financial loss, the end of a powerful relationship, or a change in leadership.

What does the next chapter in my life look like?
The next chapter may involve a significant transformation or shift in your sources of strength, power, or financial security (Bear). It suggests a necessary ending or change (Coffin), perhaps in your career or personal life, which will lead you to a period of growth and reassessment.

What is my current path leading me toward? Your current path is likely leading you toward an ending or transformation (Coffin) in an area where you may have felt secure or in control (Bear). This change will bring about a necessary reevaluation of your situation.

MOUNTAIN + SUN

21 Mountain
Obstacles · Challenge · Struggle
Detour · Frustration · Stagnation
Resistance · Delay · Hardship

31 Sun
Positive Energy · Success · Victory
Optimism · Achievement · Confidence
Radiance · Triumph · Impact

Together, the Mountain and Sun cards suggest that any obstacles or delays (Mountain) will eventually lead to a positive outcome or success (Sun).

How does my dog feel about being adopted? Your dog likely feels that there were some initial challenges or adjustments to overcome (Mountain), but is now experiencing joy, warmth, and happiness (Sun) in the new environment. While there may have been a period of uncertainty, the overall feeling is one of comfort, positivity, and growing connection.

Should I move to a new house? The cards suggest that while moving may come with its own set of challenges or obstacles (Mountain), the end result will bring a sense of happiness, success, and fulfillment (Sun). If you are ready to tackle the hurdles, the move could ultimately lead to a bright and positive new chapter in your life.

KEY + TOWER

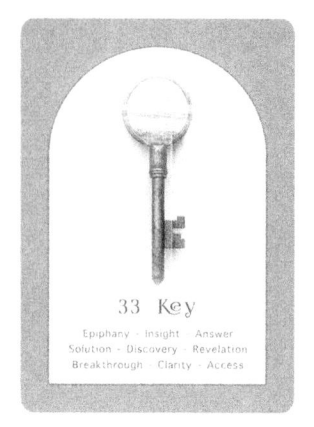

Together, the Key and Tower cards suggest that the solution or breakthrough you're seeking (Key) is linked to a place of authority, structure, or perhaps a solitary, reflective environment (Tower).

Where should I go on my next vacation? Consider a destination that offers a sense of structure, history, or solitude (Tower). A location tied to knowledge, culture, or quiet contemplation will help unlock something valuable for you (Key).

What do I need to let go of to move forward? To move forward, you may need to let go of any rigid structures, outdated authority figures, or a sense of isolation that might be holding you back (Tower). Your breakthrough may come through releasing these constraints (Key). Embrace more flexibility or personal freedom and open yourself to solutions that are not confined by rules or past limitations.

CROSS + RING

36 Cross
Burden · Responsibility · Faith
Obligation · Suffering · Spirituality
Redemption · Moral Lesson

25 Ring
Connection · Promise · Fidelity
Commitment · Partnership · Alliance
Relationship · Agreement · Union

Together, the Cross and Ring cards suggest that commitment or a contractual bond (Ring) may bring challenges or burdens (Cross). It implies that long-term commitments may require sacrifices or enduring hardship.

Should I get married? Marriage may bring significant challenges or responsibilities (Cross), requiring you to endure difficult moments. If you choose to get married, be prepared for the commitments and sacrifices that come with it (Ring). On the positive side, approaching these difficulties with a confident mindset could actually help you forge a strong marriage.

What do I need to know about my career path? Your career path may involve enduring challenges and commitments (Ring) that can feel burdensome at times (Cross). Be prepared for difficulties, but know that your dedication can lead to meaningful career growth.

SCYTHE + CHILD

Together, the Scythe and Child cards suggest that you have the need to remove or cut away (Scythe) what no longer serves you in order to make space for something new and refreshing (Child).

How can I be happier? To increase your happiness, consider making a decisive change (Scythe) that involves embracing new opportunities or starting fresh (Child). This could mean cutting away habits, relationships, or situations that no longer contribute to your well-being, and instead focusing on new beginnings or things that bring you joy.

What kind of car should I buy? You should look for a car that represents a fresh start or something different from what you've had before (Child). You should be decisive in your choice, cutting through indecision quickly (Scythe) and going for a car that feels like a new beginning.

BOUQUET + SHIP

9 Bouquet
Joy | Gratitude | Beauty
Pleasant Surprises | Gifts | Kindness
Positive Emotions | Appreciation

3 Ship
Adventure - Expansion - Departure
Journey - Exploration - New Horizons
Distance - Progress - Travel

Together, the Bouquet and Ship cards suggest that positive energy and new opportunities (Bouquet) are on the horizon, especially in areas related to growth, exploration, or expansion.

What's the current energy around my love life? The energy around your love life is positive, full of potential, and primed for progress (Ship). There is a sense of joy and fulfillment within your romantic life (Bouquet), and new experiences or connections are likely on the way.

What's blocking me from reaching my goals? The blockage in reaching your goals may be linked to a failure to explore new opportunities (Ship). While there is positivity (Bouquet), you may be held back by not taking the necessary steps to move forward or by staying too comfortable in your current situation.

Printed in Great Britain
by Amazon